"Solonche is productive and prolific, but that doesn't water down the poetry. He can compress a philosophical treatise into three lines... His epigrammatic tidy poems are philosophic gems. Solonche sees humor and encapsulates it; he frames a thought in perfect verse... He's playful and profound — the more he writes, the more he seems to know. Beneath the Solonche simplicity are significant social comments, and his goodwill reinforces the best in us."

— Grace Cavalieri, *Washington Independent Review of Books*

"Solonche, an accomplished poet, employs various forms in this compilation, including haiku, prose poem, and free verse. The poems often imaginatively enter into the natural or material world via anthropomorphic similes... Many works have an aphoristic quality that recall Zen koans, and they can be playfully amusing or even silly... A strong set of sympathetic but never sentimental observations."

— *Kirkus Reviews*

"The spirit of Horace, the melancholy of time slithering away and turning all to dust, tempered with art, wit, and good grace..."

— Ricardo Nirenberg, editor of *Offcourse: A Literary Journal*

"In a style that favors brevity and pith, J.R. Solonche brings a richness of experience, observation, and wit into his poems. Here is the world! they exclaim. And here, and here, and here! Watched over by ancient lyric gods – Time, Death, and Desire — we find the quotidian here transformed."

— Christopher Nelson, editor of Green Linden Press

"Solonche is at home with himself, "even at home," as he declares in one of his poems. His witty and matter of fact reporting of the simple observations invites us in. It is a pleasure for us to visit him in these poems. They are clouds in the sky of his mind; rich in their shapes and in their subtle colors. His poem *Dreams* reads: *Only in / the best / of dreams / is there / no such thing / as a dream.* Similarly, in his poems, he reaches a place where there is no such thing anymore as a poem."

— Korkut Onaran

Enjoy Yourself

J.R. Solonche

SERVING
HOUSE
BOOKS

Enjoy Yourself

Copyright © 2020 by J.R. Solonche

All Rights Reserved

Published by Serving House Books

Copenhagen, Denmark and South Orange, NJ

www.servinghousebooks.com

ISBN: 978-1-947175-21-1

Library of Congress Control Number: 2020930129

Member of The Independent Book Publishers Association

First Serving House Books Edition 2020

Cover Design: J.R. Solonche

Author Photograph: Emily Solonche

Serving House Books Logo: Barry Lereng Wilmont

BOOKS BY J.R. SOLONCHE

The Time of Your Life
For All I Know
The Porch Poems
To Say the Least
A Public Place
True Enough
If You Should See Me Walking on the Road
I, Emily Dickinson & Other Found Poems
The Jewish Dancing Master
Tomorrow, Today, and Yesterday
In Short Order
Heart's Content
Invisible
The Black Birch
Won't Be Long
Beautiful Day
Peach Girl: Poems for a Chinese Daughter (with Joan I. Siegel)

CONTENTS

Home 11
A Small Cloud 12
Opinions 13
Suddenly 14
Barely 15
You Must Go Away to Stay Where You Are 16
The Bare Maximum 17
The Year Begets September 18
Testimony 19
Very Short Ode on My Zippo Lighter 20
Today I Saw the Car of My Heart's Desire 21
Merriment 22
Soteriology 23
It Is Not So Hard 24
This Morning I Saw Sunshine 25
The Difference 26
The Black Hole 27
I Wish 28
In the Hydrangea 29
Unambiguous Ambivalence 30
A House 31
Where in the World 32
Let's Play the Sin Like the Violin 33
I Just Read an Awful Poem 34
I've Always Wanted to Write 35
September 36
How Do You Talk to a Person 37
Princess SummerFallWinterSpring 38
In the Parking Lot 39
It Is Said 40
There Are Times I Am So Tired of Myself 41
False Modesty 42
Without the Breeze 43
A Butterfly 44
A Noiseless Impatient Spider 45

The Ides of September 46
One Way of Looking at Thirteen Blackbirds 47
I Placed Tennessee in a Jar 48
Bless It All to Heaven! 49
Single Files 50
A Coupling 51
Sleeping Potion 52
Proximity 53
My Art Suffers for Me 54
Leave the Lingual to the Linguists, the Language to the Languagists 55
The Owl 56
Quantum Poem 57
I Have Just Eaten 58
Immoral Equivalence 59
When the Dark 60
Three Cars 61
The Mind 62
Somebody 63
A Sequence of Consequences 64
Enjoy Yourself 65
Dreams 66
I Was Certain 67
In All the Dreams 68
Tell Me Again 69
The Yellow 70
In the Bar 71
Enough 72
We Were Talking about Movies 73
Swamp 75
On My Lap 76
Wisteria 77
In the Trees 78
Supermarket 79
The Concert 80
Words 81
My Neighbor's Wife 82
Immateriality Is Still Reality 83
Dialogue 84
A & Q 85
Tranquility Recollected in Thoughts 86
My Favorite Place to Write 87

I Met a Former Student 88
Somebody Came Up to Me 89
It Was in Front 90
I Went into Bank Square 91
How Do You Want to Die? 92
The Sky Should Be Sacrosanct 93
To My Elbows 94
To My Knees 95
The Girl Who Answered the Phone 96
A Philosopher's Stone 97
Go Out and Listen to the Frogs 98
Behind Me the Sunset Is Speaking 99
Diogenes Said 100
Rhetorical Answer 101
Acknowledgments 102
About the Author 103

HOME

We are so adaptable,
so adaptable,

that no matter where
we find ourselves,

we manage to make
ourselves at home,

even at home,
even there.

A SMALL CLOUD

A small cloud drifts overhead.
The cloud is actually eight small clouds.
It is an island chain of clouds.
Soon it evaporates.
Soon it disappears.
I must remember this when I am asked,
"What is the soul?"

OPINIONS

"Act your age,"
one said.

"You're only as old as you feel,"
another said.

I'm looking
for a tie-breaker.

SUDDENLY

Suddenly, a hundred
blackbirds cracked out
of the trees into the open
as though a long shadow long
in the shadows was free to go.

BARELY

Barely visible
just barely in
the blue, the moon,
like a slender bit
of white cloud,
is just enough up
there to keep up
keeping it up.

YOU MUST GO AWAY TO STAY WHERE YOU ARE

That is a given.
That was given as a gift.

That was a gift from the goddess of gift-giving.
She is the very same who gives us this day.

She is the very same who giveth and taketh away.
You must go as far away as possible to stay as long.

There is no other possibility to belong.
No posse will ever be sent to find you.

No posse will ever be sent to bring you back to face justice.
You will face the music, for the music is everywhere of the spheres.

You must go into the mist of the mountains.
You must go into the echo of the canyon.

You must go to the south sea atoll.
You will not be found there at all.

You must go to the city of the million.
You must go to the desert of the single numbers.

You must go to the forest of the acorn gatherers.
You must go to the plateau places.

You must go to the jugular of the jungle.
You must go far, far away to stay where you are.

You must go to the moon.
Oh, no, you must not, for there you will be found real soon.

You must go to the farthest far away star.
To the farthest far away star you must go to stay forever where you are.

THE BARE MAXIMUM

At most, it is
the least
you can do.

THE YEAR BEGETS SEPTEMBER

The year begets September.
September begets two yellows.
The leaves come yellow down the wild cherry trees.
The school buses come yellow out the bus garages.

TESTIMONY

I want to testify.
I want to give an opening statement.
I want to answer questions for the record.
I want to place my left hand on the bible even though I don't believe in it.
I want to raise my right hand.
I want to swear to tell the truth.
I want to swear to tell the whole truth.
I want to swear to tell nothing but the truth.
I want to swear so help me god even though I don't believe in it.
I want to do this officially in the presence of officials.
I want to prove a poet can tell the truth.
I want to prove a poet can tell the whole truth.
I want to prove a poet can tell nothing but the truth.
I want to prove a poet can do this without telling it slant.
I want to tell what I saw.
I want to tell what I heard.
I want to tell what I know for sure.
I want the bastard to go to prison for life without parole.
I want the mother fucker to die in prison because I put him there.

VERY SHORT ODE ON MY ZIPPO LIGHTER

O, fire-breather dragon!
O, brushed chrome companion!
How faithful to me when we smoked.
How you never failed to light my cigarette.
How you never failed to light the cigarette of the lady in the restaurant.
I have you still although you've lost your spark.
I have you still although your fire is out.
I have you still to remind me of those bygone days of chivalry.
O, brushed chrome companion!
O, fire-breather dragon!

TODAY I SAW THE CAR OF MY HEART'S DESIRE

Today I saw the car of my heart's desire.
It was a Bentley.
It was in the lot of the used car dealer on Route 300.
It was white.
It was a convertible.
It was used, but it looked brand new.
It was white.
It was so white, my eyes hurt.
The chrome sparkled in the sunlight.
The chrome gleamed in the sunlight.
The chrome sparkled and gleamed and made my eyes numb in the sunlight.
It was the whitest white I've ever seen.
It was the chromiest chrome I've ever seen.
It was love at first sight.
I could not feel my eyes.
I will not buy it.
But I will kill him who does.
Then I will destroy it.
Then I will go to prison for the rest of my life.

MERRIMENT

I laughed to myself
when I heard them
laugh out loud about
a secret joke until, out
of ear shot, I laughed out
loud at my secret joke
louder than they laughed.

SOTERIOLOGY

My system of salvation
is simple, so simple,
it is simply this.
A dimple.
A kiss.

IT IS NOT HARD

It is not hard
to become hard.
It does not take
very much. All
it takes is one
small soft spot
in the center of
the chest close
to the heart. But
careful. Not in it.

THIS MORNING I SAW SUNSHINE

This morning I saw sunshine
all in black walking a dog
on the path around the lake.
I saw sunshine's hair was up.
I saw sunshine's lips were red.
I saw sunshine's ears were tiny
diamonds. I saw sunshine's smile
blind me, so I stopped and turned
to see if sunshine was really
sunshine that I saw all in black
with a dog on the path around
the lake, and it was, it was, it was,
for O, I could not bear to think
it was not sunshine but only a blonde.

THE DIFFERENCE

between rock
and stone is
not geology.
It is how much
you can carry
in one hand.

THE BLACK HOLE

at the center of poetry
wants to suck all the words
down into it. Fortunately,
the Chinese invented paper.

I WISH

I wish god existed so
I could hear him laugh.
I cannot think of any other
reason to wish god existed.

IN THE HYDRANGEA

In the hydrangea,
one savage butterfly
salvages what's left
of summer.

UNAMBIGUOUS AMBILVALENCE

First I thought it would need to make sense someday.
Then I thought it would never need to make sense.

First I sensed I would need to be thoughtful someday.
Then I sensed I would never need to be thoughtful.

First I believed you would have to believe me someday.
Then I believed you would never have to believe me.

First I figured I would figure it out someday.
Then I figured I would never figure it out.

First I realized I would realize the truth someday.
Then I realized I would never realize the truth.

First I concluded that I would come to a conclusion someday.
Then I concluded that I would never come to a conclusion.

First I decided that I would reach a decision someday.
Then I decided that I would never reach a decision.

A HOUSE

Is a house a home?
Is a home sweet?
Is a home where you hang your hat?
If a house is not a home, what is?
Can a room be a home?
Can a room in a house that is not a house be a home?
Is it a heart?
The heart can be a home to many things.
The heart can be a home to many belongings.
But the heart can be a home to only one long longing.
The heart can be the home to one long longing that never leaves.
Is the lady of the house at home?
Is the man of the house at home?
Is the lady of the house wearing a blue blouse?
Is the man of the house a louse?
Is the lady of the house his spouse?
Is the man of the house her spouse?
Is the lady of the house chasing a mouse?
Is the man of the house a souse?
Is the lady of the house wearing no blouse?
Does the man of the house do nothing all day but grouse?
The heart is the house where the one long longing that never leaves is at
home.
The heart is the world's most expensive house.
The heart is the world's smallest house.

WHERE IN THE WORLD

Where in the world is Where in the World?
Is it on the other side of the world?
Is it in China?
Is it in India?
Is it in Mongolia?
Is it here?
Are we on the other side of the world?
Whose side are we on?
The light side or the dark side?
Aren't the stars always there even if you cannot see them
because the sun is in the way?
Whose side are we on anyway?

LET'S PLAY THE SIN LIKE THE VIOLIN

Let's play the sin like the violin.
Let it begin in the dark and end in the stratosphere.
Let only the angels hear.
Let's take it on the chin.
They will lose.
We will win.
Let only the angels stare.

I JUST READ AN AWFUL POEM

I just read an awful
poem about a yellow leaf
that the speaker mistakes
for a yellow butterfly. I'm
waiting to read the good
one in which a yellow
butterfly mistakes a yellow
leaf for a yellow butterfly
and tries to mate with it.

I'VE ALWAYS WANTED TO WRITE

I've always wanted to write
a poem about Freud. I don't
know why, but it's probably
because I repressed a dream
I had about it. Anyway, my
favorite Freud story is what
he said about the Irish, that
they were the only people who
could not be psychoanalyzed.
He never explained why, but
I have the explanation. The Irish
cannot be psychoanalyzed
because they are natural poets,
and poets, as we all know,
wear their psyches on their sleeves
already for all the world to readily
see. This came to me in a dream.

SEPTEMBER

The small white flowers
are big enough to get
the bees to see them, the
same bees I have not seen
for days, the same bees
I believed were gone for good,
but the small white flowers
have brought them back again
for their own selfish reason,
for their own good. Praise to you,
small white flowers.

HOW DO YOU TALK TO A PERSON

How do you talk to a person
who looks like a corpse? How
do you exchange pleasantries?
How do you say, "What a beautiful
day?" So I say, "What a beautiful day."
How do you say, "It looks like rain?"
So I say, "It looks like rain." How
do you say, "It smells like fall"?
So I say, "It smells like fall." How
do you look her in the eye, the
neighbor who looks like a corpse?
So I look her in the eye. How do
you touch her hand and say, "Take
care. See you tomorrow?" So I touch
her hand and say, "Take care. See
you tomorrow." How do you talk
to a person who looks like death
without closing your eyes, without
exhaling the longest sigh you have
ever in your life sighed, without
crying inside so she cannot hear,
without glancing up at her husband
in the driver's seat and not let him
hear what your eyes are saying?
So I say, "What a beautiful day."

PRINCESS SUMMERFALLWINTERSPRING

I was in love with her.
I was ten, but I was in love.
I was in love, but I was ten.
She was Princess SummerFallWinterSpring.
I learned the seasons of the year from her.
I learned the seasons of myself from her.
I had wet dreams about her.
In all four seasons.
I lost my virginity to her four times in my wet dreams.
O, Princess SummerFallWinterSpring, where have you gone?
Where, O where have you gone, Princess SummerFallWinterSpring?

IN THE PARKING LOT

The woman liked my bumper sticker,
the one that reads, *Make America
Think Again.* "Thanks," I said, "but
I'm not really so sure America was
ever able to think to begin with."
"Well, Jefferson was a thinker, wasn't
he?" she said. "Yes, but he owned
slaves." "Wilson was a thinker," she
said. "Wasn't he a college president?"
"He was," I said. "But he was a racist.
He watched *The Birth of a Nation* in
the White House." "Clinton and Obama
were thinkers." "Okay," I said. "But
Clinton was impeached. And Obama,
well, I think he sometimes was too much
a thinker." "What about Carter?" she
said. "What about him?" "Didn't he
have the highest IQ of any president?"
"Yeah, I heard that, too, but he was
beaten in a landslide by that non-thinker,
Reagan. And non-thinker Bush beat
thinker Gore in 2000." "Only in the
Electoral College," she reminded me.
"Okay," I said. "But please, please,
let's not think about what happened to
thinker Hilary." "No, let's not think
about that," she said getting into her car.

IT IS SAID

It is said that all
the magnetic force
in the universe is not
equal to the force of
one magnet on the door
of your refrigerator. Is
this why I am more
attracted to my beer
than to the universe?

THERE ARE TIMES I AM SO TIRED OF MYSELF

There are times I am so tired of myself,
I try to imagine I am another species,
a moth, a frog, a crow, a skunk, but
no matter how hard I concentrate,
I never get there. I am always just
a human moth or a human frog or
a human crow or a human skunk.
The nearest I have ever come is a crow.
Caw, caw, caw, caw, caw, caw, caw.

FALSE MODESTY

I would rather have
ten false starts
than one false ending.

WITHOUT THE BREEZE

Without the breeze,
the trees have nothing to say.

Without the wind to pester their leaves,
to bother their branches,

the trees have no answers,
except for silence,

which, as in every case,
we take for "Yes."

A BUTTERFLY

A butterfly has found
a flower that a bee
has just left,
yet finds enough
still there to make
it worth what
little time it has left.

A NOISELESS IMPATIENT SPIDER

I watched it cross the patio,
a noiseless (*Why the fuck*
hasn't anyone taken Whitman
to task over this nonsensical
adjective? Are there noisy
spiders? Really? Have you ever
heard a spider make any kind
of noise while spinning its web?
Or doing anything at all? Could
he have meant "noseless?")
impatient spider in a hurry in
its chosen direction from
sunshine into shadow, from
shadow into sunshine, to get
to the gap in the shed floor.

THE IDES OF SEPTEMBER

Are upon you.
The eyes of Texas are not.
Where are the eyes of Texas?
They are upon a yellow rose.
They are upon a yellow rose in Texas.
A yellow rose is a very good thing for eyes.
So is a red rose.
So is a white rose.
I once gave a white rose to a woman.
I once gave a yellow lily to a woman.
It was not the same woman.
I never gave a red rose to anyone.
But a woman once gave a red rose to me.
The man at the airport said, "Hey, where'd ya get that there red rose?"

ONE WAY OF LOOKING AT THIRTEEN BLACKBIRDS

Call
them
crows.

I PLACED TENNESSEE IN A JAR

I did.
I found an old map of the United States.
I cut out the state of Tennessee.
I got an old mason jar.

It was bare.
Sort of.
It was gray.
Sort of.

I placed Tennessee in the jar.
I put it on the windowsill above my desk.
I did.
It took dominion there.

It did.
It's still there taking dominion.
It is.
In my expert opinion.

BLESS IT ALL TO HEAVEN!

I know of no
curse worse
than this one
times eleven.

SINGLE FILES

In the same single file
as the deer family,
a trail of deer shit
incrementally leads me
across the lawn excrementally.

A COUPLING

A couple of white
butterflies have been
spending so much
time together, have
been so inseparable
even when they separate,
they must be a white
butterfly couple.

SLEEPING POTION

It worked like a charm.
I was asleep before I knew it.
Then I was awake before I knew it.
It was ten hours later before I knew it.
I knew my dream before I knew it was a dream.
I was a charming prince, but I was not Prince Charming.
She was there, but she was no princess.
She was the step-mother, sex-starved and desperate.
It worked like a charm.
The oil had ten hours of sleep in it.
And other than kill the prissy princess, it did no harm

PROXIMITY

The orchard is next
to the cemetery.
This must be why
the honey crisp taste
so good. The crispy,
sweet dead.

MY ART SUFFERS FOR ME

My art suffers for me.
Unlike Paul Klee.

My art suffers for me.
Unlike Williams, W.C.

My art suffers for me.
Unlike cummings, e. e.

My art suffers for me.
Unlike S. Eliot, T.

LEAVE THE LINGUAL TO THE LINGUISTS, THE LANGUAGE TO THE LANGUAGISTS

So it is written.
So it is written in the dictionary.
So it must be so.
So say the lexicographers.
So write the lexiauralists.
So the shortest distance from *Ah* to *Baa* is a straight syllable.
So the time has come.
So there is no time for prevarication.
So the joint is out of time.
So, "Time, gentlemen."
So says the bartender she.
So says the tender she.
So says the slender she.
So says the ender she.
So says the rounder ender she.
So says the pride of her gender she.
So says the mender of the broken-hearted she.
So says the neither lender nor borrower be she.
So says the sender to home she.

THE OWL

The surrounded owl,
barely heard above
the sounds of the insects
all around, nevertheless
makes herself heard to me
and to the male who answers
so roundly nonchalantly.

QUANTUM POEM

This poem
is both a poem
and not a poem
at the same time.
I know this because
I wrote it and did
not write it at the
same time, and I am
both a poet and not
a poet at the same time.

I HAVE JUST EATEN

I have just eaten
the last peach
of the peach season.
It was so much
sweeter than the first
peach of the peach season.

IMMORAL EQUIVALENCE

My neighbor down the road
is target shooting. I started
to count the shots fired,
but I stopped after forty-one.
I wonder what he gets out
of it, what sort of perverted fun
it is, shooting all those bullets
into whatever he's aiming them at.
A mound of dirt, an old dead tree,
a life-size manikin six-point deer.
"Hey, Solonche, pronouncing the "e,"
what do you get out of writing
a poem?" I hear him ask me
in my mind. "Satisfaction," I hear
myself answer. *Bang, bang, bang,*
bang, bang, I hear him squeeze
them off like a crazy song he sang.

WHEN THE DARK

When the dark
rain clouds moved
over, broad banks
of bright clouds
were left above
the rain clouds'
altitude to change
the whole day's
attitude left behind.

THREE CARS

I asked the man getting out
of his Volvo in the parking lot
if he knew what the word Volvo
means. "No," he said. "What?"
"It means *I roll* in Latin," I said.
"Well, that's interesting," he said.
"What's Subaru backwards?"
"I don't know. What?" I said.
"It's U R A Bus," he said.
I laughed. "Hey, you know how
that car got its name?" I said,
pointing to a Mercedes-Benz.
"Sure," he said. "It's named for
the German guy who invented it."
"You're half right," I said. "Karl
Benz was the German guy who
invented it, but who was Mercedes?"
"His wife?" he said. "Good guess, but
no," I said. "'It's a long story," I said,
"but Mercedes was the name of the
granddaughter of a Hungarian rabbi.
It's true. You can look it up."
"No shit," he said. "You mean
Hitler's favorite car was named for
a Jewish kid?" "Yep," I said.
"That's better than I roll," he said.
"That's better than U R A Bus,"
I said. "Have a good day," he said.
"You, too," I said.

THE MIND

The mind
is the sky,
and poems
are its clouds.

SOMEBODY

Somebody must have said it.
Somebody must have known it was all about childhood.
Somebody must have known what it meant.
Somebody must have been heroic.
Somebody must have made the journey there and back.
Somebody must have defied all common sense.
Somebody must have denied the obvious.
Somebody must have disappointed his earliest teachers.
Somebody must have been left for dead.
Somebody must have been unwanted dead or alive.
Somebody must have left home too late.
Somebody must have been the nobody, too.
Somebody must have known it was high time.
Somebody must have been held up to ridicule.
Somebody must have been held to a higher standard.
Somebody must have held his breath until he turned blue.
Somebody must have said, "To hell with the stars."
Somebody must have told the angels to go fuck themselves.
Somebody must have known that only the angels could.
Somebody must have seen the moon masturbate.
Somebody must have known on what night it did.
Somebody must have wondered where they all had gone.
Somebody must have wandered around on his own.
Somebody must have wondered when he would be greeted.
Somebody must have wandered in the garden.
Somebody must have wondered why it is fourteen.
Somebody must have wondered where the daughter was.
Somebody must have wandered out onto the porch.
Somebody must have wondered why a quart of rain was on the porch.

A SEQUENCE OF CONSEQUENCES

I wanted to know when I could talk foolishly.
I wanted to know when I could be proud of melancholy.
I wanted to know when I could hold my own on my own.
I wanted to know when I could own up.
I wanted to know when I could own a yellow tie.
I wanted to know when I could wear a yellow tie with a purple shirt.
I wanted to know when I could sound wise.
I wanted to know when I could sound off.
I wanted to know when to hide and when to seek.
I wanted to know who was on my side.
I wanted to know who could outsmart me.

ENJOY YOURSELF

My mother's favorite song
was *Enjoy Yourself, It's Later
Than You Think*. I think it
was the only song I ever
heard her sing. She sang it
in the kitchen while cooking
dinner. She sang it while
ironing sheets and shirts
and pillow cases. She sang it
in the basement of the building
doing the laundry. And when
she wasn't singing it, she
was humming it. She hummed
it while pushing my baby
brother in his stroller which
had been mine. She hummed it
in the car on our way up to
the Catskills in the summer.
"Enjoy yourself, it's later
than you think, enjoy yourself,
it's later than you think, later
than you think, later than you,
later than, later," and she was
right, it was later than we thought,
later than all four of us thought.

DREAMS

Only in
the best

of dreams
is there

no such thing
as a dream.

I WAS CERTAIN

I was certain the monarch
butterfly caught in the draft
between the trailer trucks on
the interstate was doomed
until I saw it make its way out
and fly low over them both,
then way high over the highway.

IN ALL THE DREAMS

In all the dreams, the woman lies.
In all the dreams, the woman tells the truth.

In all the dreams, the train waits for him.
In all the dreams, the train leaves.

In all the dreams, he flies over the wires.
In all the dreams, he cannot get off the ground.

In all the dreams, he sees without glasses.
In all the dreams, he loses the glasses and falls.

In all the dreams, he commands attention.
In all the dreams, he attends to the commands.

In all the dreams, he leads the band with a rose.
In all the dreams, he is led by the nose.

In all the dreams, the woman lies.
In all the dreams, the woman tells the truth.

TELL ME AGAIN

Tell me again
what I was told

when I was young
what poetry is

supposed to do.
I am old.

I am old.
I have forgotten.

THE YELLOW

chrysanthemums
are about as yellow
as yellow gets,
but a leaf fallen
from a tree behind
me taps my shoulder
falling to remind me
it is there.

IN THE BAR

"Did you see *Bohemian Rhapsody*,"
I asked the barmaid. "You know,
the movie?" "Yes, I did," she said.
"Did you cry?" "Yes, a little. It was
sad. What happened to him was sad.
Did you cry?" "Yes, I cried a lot."
"Well, you're a poet, so you're
supposed to cry." "But are we poets
supposed to cry a lot?" "Yes, oh yes,
you are," she said. "A lot." "And why
is that?" I asked. "So we don't have to,"
she said putting my beer on the bar.

ENOUGH

With flowers enough
to keep both of them
busy, the butterflies
and the bees know
what it means to coexist,
or just to be oblivious.

WE WERE TALKING ABOUT MOVIES

We were talking about movies.
Soon it got around to movies about
poets. *Beautiful Dreamers* is one
about Whitman. *Bright Star* about Keats.
A Quiet Passion about Dickinson.
Tom and Viv about Eliot and his wife.
Shakespeare in Love is about, well,
Shakespeare, but we agreed that he
doesn't count, and we agreed that poets
don't make good subjects for movies.
They're boring. Frost wouldn't be
good although he did threaten to kill
himself with a pistol at breakfast.
That would be a good scene. Stevens
wouldn't either despite the fact that
he was knocked down by Hemingway
at a cocktail party. Another good scene.
Bishop? Sure, she was a lesbian, but
not a good subject for a film. Boring.
Byron would be perfect for a movie.
He died in Greece fighting for their
independence. And that club foot of his.
A real challenge for Brad Pitt. Or Leo.
Bukowski did make a good subject.
An exception. An interesting movie
about a poet is *Paterson,* which is about
the hometown of William Carlos
Williams more than it's about him,
and about a bus driver in Paterson
who's a poet and whose name
is Paterson. Interesting but far
from the best. A really crazy movie
about a poet is *The Libertine* with
Johnny Depp as John Wilmot, Second
Earl of Rochester. Nothing if not

boring, especially the part where
his nose falls off from syphilis.
Speaking of Johnny Depp, wouldn't
he be an absolutely great Poe?
My favorite movie about a poet has
to be *If I Were King*, starring
Ronald Colman as Francois Villon.
And my favorite line (screenplay by
Preston Sturges) has to be this: "No
offense. Poetry is its own worst enemy."
Mais où sont les neiges d'antan?

SWAMP

Where yesterday
three turtles sunned
themselves on a log,
today I saw a log
three-turtles long.

ON MY LAP

I could have a cat on my lap.
But I don't.

I could have a grandchild on my lap.
But I don't.

I could have a shotgun on my lap.
But I don't.

I could have a woolen blanket on my lap.
But I don't.

I could have a Jane Austen novel on my lap.
But I don't.

I could have a lap dancer on my lap.
But I don't.

Instead I have my pal, my notebook looking up at me
with that blank stare from my lap on my lap.

WISTERIA

The wisteria,
long dead,
nevertheless, holds on,
in its death-grip,
to its host tree for dear life.

IN THE TREES

In the tress
behind me,

there is a bird
whose call

sounds like
a kiss.

It must be a love bird.
Or a Cosa Nostra bird.

SUPERMARKET

In the supermarket, a woman
was pushing a shopping cart
with a dog sitting in it. There
was nothing else in the shopping
cart. The dog was so big, it took
up just about the whole thing.
I encountered her three or four
times in different aisles, and she
still hadn't bought anything.
I got the distinct impression that
she was in the store for no other
reason than to show off the dog.
I can certainly understand why.
The dog was beautiful all right,
very beautiful, even stunningly
beautiful. "What kind?" I asked
after our fourth meeting. "She's
a husky and shepherd mix," she
said. "She's beautiful," I said.
"Thank you," she said. Jesus,
she was the only dog I ever saw
that I wanted to marry.

THE CONCERT

It was boring.
It was Bach's Cantata #18.

It was boring.
"Just as the rain and snow fall from heaven"

It was boring as the rain.
It was boring as the snow.

It was boring as heaven.
There were other baroque pieces.

They were boring.
William Byrd was boring.

That other guy was boring.
I can't believe what I'm saying.

Bach was boring.
My beloved Bach was boring.

The closest thing in my book to divinity,
and he was boring.

Oh, god, he was so boring.
As boring as god.

WORDS

Were there words?
If there were, were words exchanged?
Which words got the short end of the stick?
Was there a conversation?
Was there a monologue?
Was there a dialogue?
Were the words whispered?
Were the words shouted?
Were the words read on your lips?
Were the words polite?
Were the words civil?
Were the words heated?
Were the words red in the face?
Were the words white hot?
Were the words dirty?
Were the words appropriate for mixed company?
Were the words of four letters?
Were the words off-color?
Were the words Anglo-Saxon?
Did the words rhyme?
Did the words enjoy themselves in your mouth?
Which of the words was as good as your bond?
Were the words put into your mouth?
Were the words taken right out of your mouth?
Which of the words did you have to eat?
Which of the words did you have to spit out?
Were the words names?
Did the names never hurt you?
Which of the words did you stand by?
Which of the words was Hamlet reading?
Which of the words did the Greeks have for it?
Which of the words was the First Word?
Which of the words was the Last Word?
Which of your words can I take for it?
Which of my words can you take for it?

MY NEIGHBOR'S WIFE

My neighbor's wife
passed away a week ago.
She was two years younger
than I am. It was a heart
attack. It was sudden. It
happened "just like that,"
Harvey said. I'm going
for my daily walks around
the lake at noon now, or
as close to noon as I can,
when no shadow is on
the road ahead of me or
behind me, or when it
is the shortest shadow.

IMMATERIALITY IS STILL REALITY

You can call it a cloud.
You can call it a mist or a fog or a haze.
You can call it illusion.
You can call it delusion.
You can call it the conspiracy of cortex chemistry.
Call it what you will.
What you call it is immaterial.
Immateriality is still reality.

DIALOGUE

"Hey, what are you writing about?"
asks my daughter. "The chrysanthemums?"
"No," I say. "The leaves falling?" "No,"
I say. "This perfect fall day?" "No," I say.
"I'm waiting," I say. "For what?" she
asks. "For something to write about,"
I say. "Like what?" she asks. "Well, for
something like the chrysanthemums but
not the chrysanthemums. For something
like the leaves falling but not the leaves
falling. For something like this perfect
fall day but not this perfect fall day."
"Okay," she says. "Good luck." "Thanks,"
I say. Whenever I'm just waiting around,
I can always count on my daughter.

A & Q

"I feel like a failure if
I don't write every day,"
someone said to the famous
poet after the reading."You
feel like a failure at what?
At writing poetry? Or at being
a poet?" asked the famous poet.
"Is there a difference? I didn't
know," the someone said. "You
do now," said the famous poet.

TRANQUILITY RECOLLECTED IN THOUGHTS

Is there another way?
Is there another way to recollect tranquility?

Yes, there is.
There is another way

to recollect tranquility.
In bars.

MY FAVORITE PLACE TO WRITE

My favorite place
to write is outside.
I have to be outside.
I have to be under
the sky. I have to be
under the sun. I have
to be under the clouds.
I have to be under the stars.
It looks like I will have
to move to Arizona.

I MET A FORMER STUDENT

I met a former student.
I didn't recognize him.
He recognized me. It
always happens that way.
I never recognize them.
They always recognize me.
I've had so many over
the years. Thousands.
I remember so few. Only
the extraordinary ones.
Like the one who went
on to become a professor
at Vassar College.
Son-of-a-bitch.

SOMEBODY CAME UP TO ME

Somebody came up to me
after the reading. "You write
too many poems about poetry,"
he said. "Really?" I said.
"Yeah," he said. "Too many
poems about writing poetry."
"Gee," I said. "I hadn't realized
that. Thanks for telling me.
But, you know, it's what I know
about more than anything else,
so it's natural that I write about
what I know about the most.
Is that bad?" "Well, it's not
bad exactly," he said. "So
what's the problem?" I asked.
"Well, you know, you should
write about other things," he
said. "Like what?" I said. "Well,"
he said. (He said "well" a lot.)
"Sunsets. Mountains. Birds.
Autumn leaves. Love." "Thanks
for the suggestion," I said. "But
I'll leave that to you."

IT WAS IN FRONT

It was in front of the Zion
Baptist Church on Main.
It was parked between
two long black limousines.
The most beautiful hearse I've ever seen.
It looked brand new,
looked like it was just driven
out of the hearse showroom.
The three were so polished, so glossy,
they sparkled like onyx rings.
They made the sunlight do soft shoe
on the roofs and hoods.
They made the sunshine sing
the blues in the night fields of Mississippi.

I WENT INTO BANK SQUARE

I went into Bank Square
Coffee for coffee.
The television was on.
The president was on.
I gave the screen the finger.
I looked around. No one
was watching. Everyone
had their heads down.
Their heads were down.
Down, down were their
heads into their own
little screens. "This explains
everything," I said out loud.
No one looked up. No one
heard me, for all the heads
were down, down, down.
"Shit, this will explain
everything," I said to myself.
The coffee was good.
The best in town.

HOW DO YOU WANT TO DIE?

Do you want to die
in your sleep in bed?
I want to die under a blue sky.

Do you want to die suddenly?
Do you want to die without warning?
I want to die under a blue sky.

I want to die in my sleep.
I want to die in the middle
of a dream about being born.

Twice I want to die.
I want to die dreaming about being born.
And again next morning under a blue sky.

THE SKY SHOULD BE SACROSANCT

The sky should be sacrosanct.
Only the birds should know it.
And the clouds when crossing over it.
And the rain and the snow when letting go of it.
The sky should be sacrosanct.
Only the sun should rule it by day.
Only the moon and stars should rule it by night.
No others must there be.
The engines there above me, they ought not be.
The sky should be free of them, the gross machines.
They should all, all be felled.
The sky should be free.
The sky should be sacrosanct.
May the Wright Brothers burn in hell.

TO MY ELBOWS

How many times, when
in a crowd, have I heard,
"They're so sharp!" about
you. Sharp as tacks, I'd say,
the way you get me through
to the front of things. And
let's not forget how I bend
you in bars to the perfect
angle of support, equilaterally
poised in three-point pose,
sometimes painfully acute,
but always right, always right.

TO MY KNEES

How have you lasted so long?
Knees, you are seventy-three years
old, and you're still going strong.
You have never locked, never seized
up. I have no complaints about you.
You're not a pain in the neck. So
unlike my hips who live above you
and are awake all night making noise.
So unlike my shoulders who constantly
complain about the cold. Knees,
nothing seems to bother you. I'm lucky
I suppose. Let me count my blessings –
one, two knees, one, two knees with wings.

THE GIRL WHO ANSWERED THE PHONE

The girl who answered the phone
at the plumbing contractor said
I sounded like a happy person, and she
liked that. "Well," I said. "I'm happy
that you think I sound like a happy
person and are happy about it. But
I have to tell you something. I'm not
a happy person." "Really?" she said.
"How come?" "I'm a poet. Poets
aren't happy people," I said. "I don't
know any poets, so I couldn't say one
way or another. But you do sound happy.
You really do." She laughed. "You sound
like a happy poet." "That's an oxymoron,"
I said. "What's an ox-ee-mor-on?" She
stopped laughing. "An oxymoron is
a phrase with an adjective and a noun
that don't agree. They contradict one
another," I said. "*Jumbo shrimp* is a
good example." "Or a sad clown? Is that
an oxymoron?" "Yes," I said. "That's
a really good one." "Well," she said.
"I still think you sound like a happy
person, or poet or whatever you are.
And I still like it." "Me, too," I said.
Then I made the appointment for the
plumber just like any happy person would.

A PHILOSOPHER'S STONE

The philosopher Zhao Li was born with an empty place beneath his heart. The wind came to fill the empty place beneath his heart, but Zhao Li said, *I am saving it for something else,* and sent the wind away. The sun came to fill the empty place beneath his heart, but Zhao Li said, *I am saving it for something else,* and sent the sun away. The clouds came to fill the empty place beneath his heart, but Zhao Li said, *I am saving it for something else,* and sent the clouds away. The rain came to fill the empty place beneath his heart, but Zhao Li said, *I am saving it for something else,* and sent the rain away. The moon came to fill the empty place beneath his heart, but Zhao Li said, *I am saving it for something else,* and sent the moon away. The sea came to fill the empty place beneath his heart, but Zhao Li said, *I am saving it for something else,* and sent the sea away. The mountain came to fill the empty place beneath his heart, but Zhao Li said, *I am saving it for something else,* and sent the mountain away. At last, when Zhao Li was a very old man, a little stone came to fill the empty place beneath his heart, and Zhao Li said, *Come, little stone, I have saved this empty place beneath my heart just for you.* So the philosopher Zhao Li died with the stone of his dreams buried beneath his heart.

GO OUT AND LISTEN TO THE FROGS

Go out and listen to the frogs, he said.
They speak for you.

So I went out to listen to the frogs
as he said, for he was a poet and spoke

with passion and audacious authority.
And in the moonlight at the pond,

I listened to the frogs speaking to one another,
and after a while I decided that the frogs

were not speaking for me but for themselves,
and after a little while longer,

I decided that I wanted the moonlight
to speak for me instead of the frogs,

the moonlight which was so much louder
than the frogs, the moonlight

which was not confined to seasonal speaking
but which spoke through the year,

the moonlight which was so much clearer
than the frogs, so much colder and more silver.

So I went out to the moon-pond and listened
to the moonlight speak for me.

And now, when they ask me, I will answer,
with passion of my own, and with my own

audacious authority: *Go out and listen to the moon.*
It speaks for you.

BEHIND ME THE SUNSET IS SPEAKING

Behind me the sunset is speaking.
"Listen carefully," it says.
"I am speaking from the heart."

Behind me a bird is speaking.
"Listen carefully," it says.
"I am speaking from the heart."

Behind me an insect is speaking.
"Listen carefully," it says.
"I am speaking from the heart."

Behind me a tree is speaking.
"Listen carefully," it says.
"I am speaking from the heart."

Behind me the breeze is speaking.
"Listen carefully," it says.
"I am speaking from the heart."

Behind me the lake is speaking.
"Listen carefully," it says.
"I am speaking from the heart."

"But that is the way you always speak,"
I say to the sunset, to the bird, to the insect,
to the tree, to the breeze, to the lake.

Behind me the sunset, the bird, the insect,
the tree, the breeze, the lake say, "Listen carefully.
We are laughing at you from the heart."

DIOGENES SAID

Diogenes said to Alexander,
Do not stand between
me and the sun.
I must remember
this when the last doctor
stands between the sun
outside the hospital room
and me in my bed
just before I'm dead.

RHETORICAL ANSWER

All things
end up

winding
down.

ACKNOWLEDGMENTS

Right Hand Pointing: One Sentence Poems

"Home"

"Suddenly"

ABOUT THE AUTHOR

J.R. Solonche is the author of 17 books of poetry and coauthor of another. He lives in the Hudson Valley.

CPSIA information can be obtained
at www.ICGtesting.com
Printed in the USA
FSHW011644041220

9 781947 175211